Firefighter

Copyright © QEB Publishing, Inc. 2009

Published in the United States by
QEB Publishing, Inc.
3 Wrigley, Suite A
Irvine, CA 92618

www.qeb-publishing.com

Library of Congress Cataloging-in-Publication Data

Askew, Amanda.
   Firefighter / by Amanda Askew ; illustrated by
Andrew Crowson.
        p. cm. -- (QEB people who help us)
   ISBN 978-1-59566-992-6 (hardcover)
  1. Fire fighters--Juvenile literature. I. Crowson,
Andrew. II. Title.
   HD8039.F5A85 2010
   363.37--dc22

2009001990

ISBN 978-1-59566-691-8 (paperback)

Printed and bound in China

Words in **bold** are explained in the glossary on page 24.

Author Amanda Askew
Designer and Illustrator Andrew Crowson
Consultants Shirley Bickler and Tracey Dils

Publisher Steve Evans
Creative Director Zeta Davies
Managing Editor Amanda Askew

Firefighter

Amanda Askew
Andrew Crowson

QEB

QEB Publishing

Meet Jack. He is a firefighter.
He helps to keep places safe
from fires. He also puts out fires.

Jack arrives at the fire station
and changes into his uniform.

At the fire station, Jack wears a blue uniform. When there is a fire alarm, Jack puts on a fire suit, a helmet, and heavy black boots.

His uniform lets people know that he is a firefighter.

Joe, the **Watch Manager**, checks that all six firefighters are there.

First, Jack and the other firefighters have to make sure that everything is working properly before the next **alarm bell** goes off.

"Everyone's here. Let's start checking and cleaning the truck," Joe says.

Later that morning, Jack puts in a new **smoke alarm** for Mrs. Patel. He shows her how to use it properly.

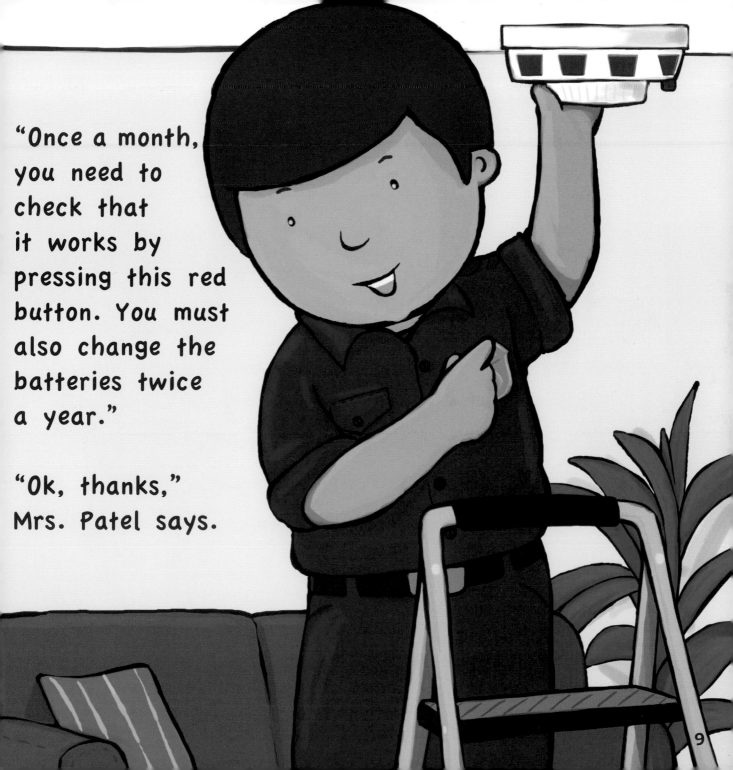

"Once a month, you need to check that it works by pressing this red button. You must also change the batteries twice a year."

"Ok, thanks," Mrs. Patel says.

Jack goes back to the station for lunch.
Just as he's finishing his sandwich...
RING, RING, RING!
It's the fire alarm.

Jack and the other firefighters
put on their helmets and rush
to the fire truck.

"Dover Street School.
There's a fire in
the kitchen!"
Joe shouts.

Jack drives and puts on the **siren** so other cars on the road will move out of the way.

When they arrive at the school, the children are standing quietly in the playground. There is smoke coming from the building.

Carl talks to the teacher
to find out what happened.

"Is anyone trapped in the building?"
Carl asks.
"No, all 75 children are out."

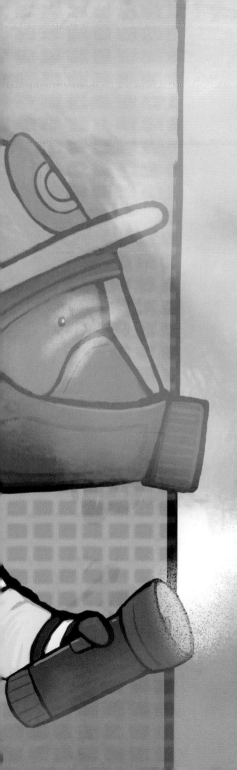

Jack, Peter, and Lucas put on **air masks** so they can breathe. They crash through the kitchen doors.

They can hardly see because the smoke is black and thick.

"Look! It's coming from the ovens." They spray water onto the flames until, at last, the fire is out.

Outside, Jack and Lucas put the hose away.

Peter and Max look to see what started the fire. They also check that the building is safe before everyone can go back inside.

"Thank you for coming so quickly," the teacher says. "Not a problem!"

Jack feels a tap on his arm. "Please, sir, can we climb on your fire truck?"

Jack laughs. "Not today. Maybe another time!"

Glossary

Air mask Something that covers your face and gives you extra air to breathe.

Alarm Equipment that makes a loud warning noise.

Siren Equipment that makes a loud warning noise. It is usually used on fire trucks and police cars.

Smoke alarm Equipment that makes a loud noise when there is smoke or fire in a building.

Station Place where firefighters work.

Uniform Type of clothing worn by firefighters.

Watch Manager The officer in charge of the fire station and the other firefighters.

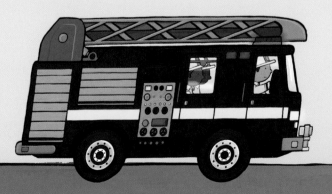

Copyright © QEB Publishing, Inc. 2009

Published in the United States by
QEB Publishing, Inc.
3 Wrigley, Suite A
Irvine, CA 92618

www.qeb-publishing.com

Library of Congress Cataloging-in-Publication Data

Askew, Amanda.
   Police officer / by Amanda Askew.
        p. cm. -- (QEB people who help us)
   ISBN 978-1-59566-989-6 (hardcover)
 1. Police--Juvenile literature. I. Title.
 HV7922.A85 2010
 363.2'2--dc22

                        2009001992

ISBN 978-1-59566-691-8 (paperback)

Printed and bound in China

Words in bold are explained in the glossary on page 24.

Author Amanda Askew
Designer and Illustrator Andrew Crowson
Consultants Shirley Bickler and Tracey Dils

Publisher Steve Evans
Creative Director Zeta Davies
Managing Editor Amanda Askew

Police Officer

Amanda Askew
Andrew Crowson

QEB
QEB Publishing

Meet Anita. She is a police officer. She helps to **prevent crime** and keep people safe.

At 7 o'clock, Anita arrives at the **police station** and changes into her **uniform**.

Anita's hat, suit, and badge make up her uniform. Her uniform lets people know that she is a police officer.

In the morning, the officers have a meeting with the **sergeant**.

He tells them about any crimes that have happened and what their jobs are today.

Anita goes out **on patrol**
in the town.

The **traffic** is very busy outside
the local school, and the
children cannot cross the road.

Anita stands in the road and holds
up her hand to stop the cars.

"I don't want you to be late for school!"
"Thanks, Officer."

Then, Anita gets a message on her radio. Some computer games have been stolen from a store on Hall Street.

10

When Anita arrives,
the storekeeper
is waiting outside.

"Officer, two boys stole
some computer games."
"Please start from the beginning
and tell me what happened."

The storekeeper tells Anita that one boy asked him for help, while the other boy put the computer games in his T-shirt. When the storekeeper saw this, the boys ran away.

"What did they look like?"
"One boy was wearing a
red T-shirt. The other
boy had red hair.
He was wearing
a purple T-shirt."

13

Back at the station, Anita calls the local school to see if anyone is absent today.

"Thomas and Ross Green aren't at school."
"Thanks, Miss Nakata. I'll go over to see their parents."

On Anita's way to the Green's home, the car in front of her doesn't stop when the traffic lights turn red.

POLICE

Anita turns on her **siren** and follows the car. This tells the driver to stop.

"Why didn't you stop at the traffic light?"
"I'm sorry, Officer. I was trying to swat a wasp. I didn't see the traffic light turn red."

"You could have caused an **accident**. Next time, pull over to the side of the road and stop the car first."

Outside the boys' house, Anita sees Ross and Thomas.

"Thomas! Ross! I think we need to talk, don't you? Let's go inside and speak to your parents."

21

Anita talks to the boys and their parents. The boys admit that they took the games.

"**Stealing** is wrong. People can go to **jail** for it. Instead, we'll take the games back to the store and tell the owner that you're sorry."

Glossary

Accident A car crash.

Jail A place where people who break the law are kept.

On patrol When a police officer walks around to make sure there is no crime.

Police station A place where police officers work.

Prevent crime To stop someone from doing something that is against the law.

Radio Equipment that is used to send spoken messages.

Sergeant An important person in the police force.

Siren Equipment that makes a loud warning noise.

Stealing Taking something that isn't yours.

Traffic Cars, buses, and other vehicles on the road.

Uniform A type of clothing worn by police officers.

"Yes, Officer. We are very sorry. We'll never do it again."

23